The Civil Rights Act

American history, Volume 11

Michael Johnson

Published by Harmony House Publishing, 2024.

THE CIVIL RIGHTS ACT

First edition. April 4, 2024.

ISBN: 979-8224294367

Written by Michael Johnson.

Table of Contents

"To those who marched, protested, and tirelessly fought for civil rights; to those whose names are etched in the annals of history and to those whose names remain unsung heroes; to the activists, leaders, and everyday individuals who dared to dream of a more just and equitable society. This book is dedicated to your courage, resilience, and unwavering commitment to equality. May the lessons of the Civil Rights Act inspire future generations to continue the march toward justice and freedom for all."

Chapter 1: Introduction

The Civil Rights Act of 1964 stands as one of the most significant pieces of legislation in American history, marking a pivotal moment in the ongoing struggle for racial equality. Enacted on July 2, 1964, after years of tireless activism and political maneuvering, the Civil Rights Act represented a landmark achievement in the fight against institutionalized racism and segregation. This chapter provides a comprehensive overview of the act, its historical context, and its enduring impact on American society.

Overview of the Civil Rights Act of 1964

The Civil Rights Act of 1964 was a sweeping piece of legislation that aimed to address and dismantle racial discrimination in various spheres of American life. Its passage marked the culmination of years of civil rights activism, legal battles, and political mobilization. The act itself consisted of several key provisions, each aimed at combating different forms of racial injustice:

1. Title I: Voting Rights: Title I of the Civil Rights Act aimed to address longstanding barriers to African American voting rights, particularly in the South. It prohibited the use of literacy tests and other discriminatory voter registration practices that had been used to disenfranchise African American voters.

2. Title II: Public Accommodations: Title II prohibited discrimination in public accommodations, such as hotels, restaurants, and theaters, based on race, color, religion, or national origin. This provision sought to end the widespread practice of segregation in public spaces and ensure equal access for all Americans.

3. Title III: Desegregation of Public Facilities: Title III extended the federal government's authority to withhold funds from programs and facilities that practiced racial segregation, such as schools and public transportation systems. It provided mechanisms for enforcing desegregation orders and promoting integration in public facilities.

4. Title IV: Desegregation of Public Education: Title IV built upon the landmark Supreme Court decision in Brown v. Board of Education (1954) by authorizing the federal government to withhold funding from school districts that maintained racially segregated schools. It aimed to accelerate the desegregation process and ensure equal educational opportunities for all students.

5. Title V: Commission on Civil Rights: Title V established the United States Commission on Civil Rights, an independent federal agency tasked with investigating and monitoring civil rights violations. The commission played a crucial role in documenting instances of discrimination and recommending policy changes to address systemic injustices.

Together, these provisions represented a comprehensive effort to address the pervasive racial discrimination that had long plagued American society. By targeting key areas such as voting rights, public accommodations, and education, the Civil Rights Act sought to dismantle the legal framework of segregation and pave the way for a more inclusive and equitable society.

Importance of the Act in American History

The significance of the Civil Rights Act of 1964 cannot be overstated. It represented a fundamental shift in American law and society, challenging centuries of entrenched racism and discrimination. By outlawing segregation and discrimination in various aspects of public life, the act struck a decisive blow against the Jim Crow system that had enforced racial hierarchy and inequality in the South and beyond.

Moreover, the Civil Rights Act of 1964 had far-reaching implications beyond its immediate legal effects. It served as a catalyst for subsequent civil rights legislation, including the Voting Rights Act of 1965 and the Fair Housing Act of 1968, which further expanded protections against racial discrimination. The act also inspired other marginalized groups to organize and demand equal rights, laying the groundwork for movements for women's rights, LGBTQ+ rights, disability rights, and more.

Furthermore, the Civil Rights Act of 1964 had a profound impact on American culture and identity. It forced the nation to confront its legacy of racism and inequality, prompting difficult conversations about privilege, power, and justice. The act inspired a new generation of activists and leaders who would continue the struggle for civil rights and social justice in the decades to come.

Preview of Key Themes and Chapters

Throughout this book, we will explore the Civil Rights Act of 1964 from multiple perspectives, examining its historical roots, legislative battles, implementation challenges, and enduring legacy. Each chapter will delve into different aspects of the act's significance, drawing on historical analysis, legal scholarship, and firsthand accounts from those who lived through this transformative period in American history.

In the following chapters, we will explore the pre-Civil Rights landscape, the origins of the Civil Rights Act, the crafting of the legislation, grassroots activism, legal challenges and Supreme Court decisions, implementation and enforcement efforts, immediate effects and reactions, the act's international influence, unfinished business in the fight for equality, commemorative efforts, contemporary perspectives, and more.

By examining the Civil Rights Act of 1964 from multiple angles, we hope to provide a comprehensive understanding of its importance as a milestone in the ongoing quest for equality and justice in America. As we embark on this journey through history, let us reflect on the struggles and triumphs of those who fought for civil rights and reaffirm our commitment to building a more inclusive and equitable society for all.

Chapter 2: Pre-Civil Rights Landscape

Before the enactment of the Civil Rights Act of 1964, the United States was deeply entrenched in a system of racial discrimination and segregation that permeated every aspect of society. This chapter explores the historical context of racial inequality, the legal framework of segregation under Jim Crow laws, and the pivotal events that laid the groundwork for the Civil Rights Movement.

Historical Context of Racial Discrimination in the United States

The roots of racial discrimination in America can be traced back to the country's colonial period and the institution of slavery. From the arrival of the first enslaved Africans in the early 17th century, African Americans were systematically deprived of their rights and subjected to brutal exploitation. Slavery not only dehumanized millions of individuals but also laid the foundation for centuries of racial hierarchy and inequality.

Even after the abolition of slavery following the Civil War and the passage of the Reconstruction Amendments (the 13th, 14th, and 15th Amendments), which granted freedom, citizenship, and voting rights to African Americans, the promise of equality remained elusive. The period of Reconstruction was short-lived, and the rise of white supremacist groups like the Ku Klux Klan, coupled with the imposition of discriminatory laws and practices, ushered in an era of segregation and disenfranchisement.

Legal Segregation and Jim Crow Laws

The term "Jim Crow" refers to a system of racial segregation and discrimination that prevailed in the Southern United States from the late 19th century until the mid-20th century. Named after a character in minstrel shows who perpetuated racist stereotypes, Jim Crow laws enforced racial segregation in public facilities, transportation, housing, employment, and education, effectively relegating African Americans to second-class citizenship.

Under Jim Crow, African Americans were subjected to a host of discriminatory practices, including:

1. Segregated Facilities: Public facilities such as schools, parks, libraries, theaters, and restaurants were segregated by race, with "whites-only" and "colored" sections or separate facilities altogether.

2. Voter Suppression: African Americans faced numerous barriers to exercising their right to vote, including poll taxes, literacy tests, grandfather clauses, and outright intimidation and violence.

3. Unequal Treatment: African Americans were denied equal access to employment opportunities, housing, healthcare, and other essential services, perpetuating economic and social disparities.

4. Violence and Terror: Lynchings, mob violence, and acts of domestic terrorism were used to maintain white supremacy and intimidate African Americans who dared to challenge the status quo.

Jim Crow laws were upheld by both state and local governments and were further reinforced by the Supreme Court's "separate but equal" doctrine established in Plessy v. Ferguson (1896), which sanctioned racial segregation as long as facilities were deemed "equal" in quality. In reality, however, facilities for African Americans were systematically underfunded and inferior to those for whites, perpetuating systemic inequality.

Pivotal Events Leading up to the Civil Rights Movement

Despite the pervasive discrimination and violence they faced, African Americans resisted oppression and fought for their rights throughout the pre-Civil Rights era. Several pivotal events and developments laid the groundwork for the emergence of the Civil Rights Movement:

1. World War II and the Double V Campaign: African American participation in World War II, both on the battlefield and on the home front, highlighted the hypocrisy of fighting for democracy abroad while facing segregation and discrimination at home. The Double V Campaign, which called for victory over fascism abroad and racism at home, galvanized support for civil rights among African American servicemen and civilians.

2. Truman's Desegregation of the Military: In 1948, President Harry Truman issued Executive Order 9981, which desegregated the U.S. armed forces and mandated equal treatment and opportunity for all service members, regardless of race. Truman's action represented a significant step toward dismantling institutionalized racism in the federal government and inspired further demands for civil rights reforms.

3. Brown v. Board of Education: The landmark Supreme Court decision in Brown v. Board of Education (1954) struck down the doctrine of "separate but equal" in public education, declaring that racially segregated schools were inherently unequal and unconstitutional. The ruling paved the way for efforts to desegregate schools nationwide and energized the nascent Civil Rights Movement.

4. Montgomery Bus Boycott: In 1955, the arrest of Rosa Parks, a Black woman who refused to give up her seat to a white passenger on a Montgomery, Alabama bus, sparked a citywide boycott of the segregated bus system. Led by Martin Luther King Jr. and other local activists, the Montgomery Bus Boycott lasted for over a year and served as a powerful example of nonviolent resistance and collective action.

These events, along with countless others, laid the foundation for the Civil Rights Movement of the 1950s and 1960s, setting the stage for the eventual passage of landmark legislation like the Civil Rights Act of 1964. As we continue to explore the history of the Civil Rights Movement and its enduring legacy, it is essential to understand the pre-Civil Rights landscape and the profound injustices that fueled the struggle for racial equality in America.

Chapter 3: Origins of the Civil Rights Act

The Civil Rights Act of 1964 did not emerge in a vacuum but was the culmination of decades of activism, legal battles, and political maneuvering aimed at dismantling racial discrimination and segregation in the United States. This chapter explores the origins of the Civil Rights Act, tracing the early attempts at civil rights legislation, highlighting influential figures and organizations advocating for change, and examining the political climate of the 1960s that propelled the push for comprehensive civil rights reform.

Early Attempts at Civil Rights Legislation

Efforts to secure civil rights for African Americans date back to the Reconstruction era following the Civil War, with the passage of the Civil Rights Act of 1866 and the ratification of the 14th and 15th Amendments to the Constitution. However, these gains were short-lived, as the rise of Jim Crow laws and systemic discrimination undermined the promise of equality for African Americans.

Throughout the late 19th and early 20th centuries, African American leaders and organizations continued to advocate for civil rights through legal challenges, grassroots activism, and public awareness campaigns. The NAACP (National Association for the Advancement of Colored People), founded in 1909, emerged as a leading force in the fight for racial justice, using litigation and advocacy to challenge segregation and discrimination in the courts and in public opinion.

Despite these efforts, progress toward civil rights legislation was slow and often met with fierce opposition from segregationist politicians and white supremacist groups. Several key legislative initiatives, including the Dyer Anti-Lynching Bill and the Fair Employment Practices Committee (FEPC), were introduced in Congress during the 1940s but ultimately failed to gain sufficient support for passage.

It was not until the post-World War II era, with the rise of the Civil Rights Movement and shifting attitudes toward race and equality, that significant momentum began to build behind the push for comprehensive civil rights reform.

Influential Figures and Organizations Advocating for Change

Numerous influential figures and organizations played pivotal roles in advocating for civil rights and laying the groundwork for the Civil Rights Act of 1964:

1. Thurgood Marshall: As the chief counsel for the NAACP Legal Defense Fund, Thurgood Marshall spearheaded the legal strategy to challenge segregation and discrimination in the courts. Marshall argued several landmark cases before the Supreme Court, including Brown v. Board of Education, which struck down racial segregation in public schools.

2. Martin Luther King Jr.: Reverend Martin Luther King Jr. emerged as a central figure in the Civil Rights Movement, advocating for nonviolent resistance and civil disobedience to challenge racial injustice. His leadership during the Montgomery Bus Boycott and the Southern Christian Leadership Conference (SCLC) helped mobilize grassroots support for civil rights reform.

3. Rosa Parks: Rosa Parks' refusal to give up her seat on a segregated bus in Montgomery, Alabama, sparked the Montgomery Bus Boycott and galvanized the Civil Rights Movement. Parks' act of defiance inspired widespread protests and drew national attention to the issue of racial segregation.

4. Ella Baker: As a key organizer and strategist within the Civil Rights Movement, Ella Baker played a crucial role in fostering grassroots leadership and empowering local communities to take action. Baker's work with the Student Nonviolent Coordinating Committee (SNCC) and other organizations helped mobilize young activists and amplify their voices.

5. A. Philip Randolph: As the founder of the Brotherhood of Sleeping Car Porters and a prominent labor leader, A. Philip Randolph advocated for both civil rights and economic justice. Randolph's efforts to organize the 1941 March on Washington for Jobs and Freedom laid the groundwork for later civil rights protests and demonstrations.

These figures, along with countless others, provided leadership, inspiration, and organizational infrastructure to the Civil Rights Movement, helping to build a broad-based coalition committed to achieving racial equality through legislative reform.

Political Climate in the 1960s Leading to the Push for Comprehensive Civil Rights Reform

The 1960s witnessed a confluence of social, political, and cultural factors that created fertile ground for the push for comprehensive civil rights reform:

1. Cold War Dynamics: The United States' position as a global superpower during the Cold War era led to increased scrutiny of its domestic policies on human rights and democracy. The Soviet Union and other communist countries highlighted racial discrimination in America as evidence of hypocrisy and moral weakness, prompting pressure for reform.

2. Media Coverage and Public Opinion: The advent of television and mass media brought images of racial injustice and civil rights protests into living rooms across America. News coverage of events such as the Birmingham campaign, the March on Washington, and the Selma to Montgomery march helped to mobilize public opinion and build support for civil rights legislation.

3. Presidential Leadership: President John F. Kennedy and later President Lyndon B. Johnson played instrumental roles in advancing civil rights legislation. Kennedy's administration supported efforts to desegregate public facilities and schools, while Johnson used his political savvy and legislative skills to shepherd the Civil Rights Act through Congress following Kennedy's assassination in 1963.

4. Civil Rights Activism: The Civil Rights Movement reached its peak in the early 1960s, with a wave of sit-ins, marches, and demonstrations across the South and beyond. The activism of grassroots organizers, student activists, religious leaders, and ordinary citizens helped to create momentum for legislative action and put pressure on lawmakers to address racial injustice.

5. National Tragedies: Tragic events such as the bombing of the 16th Street Baptist Church in Birmingham, Alabama, which killed four young girls, and the murder of civil rights activists like Medgar Evers and James Chaney, highlighted the urgent need for action to combat racial violence and discrimination.

In this charged political climate, the time was ripe for comprehensive civil rights reform. The stage was set for the introduction and passage of the Civil Rights Act of 1964, which would mark a watershed moment in American history and pave the way for further progress in the struggle for racial equality.

Chapter 4: Crafting the Legislation

The Civil Rights Act of 1964 was the product of intense congressional debates, negotiations, and compromises that spanned several years. This chapter delves into the intricacies of crafting the legislation, examining the dynamics of congressional politics, the pivotal role of President Lyndon B. Johnson in championing the bill, and the challenges and compromises that shaped its final form.

Congressional Debates and Negotiations Surrounding the Civil Rights Act

The push for comprehensive civil rights legislation faced significant opposition from Southern segregationist lawmakers, who wielded considerable influence in Congress through their seniority and committee chairmanships. For years, civil rights bills had languished in committee or been filibustered on the Senate floor, preventing meaningful progress on racial equality.

However, the tide began to turn in the early 1960s, as the Civil Rights Movement gained momentum and public opinion shifted in favor of reform. President John F. Kennedy, elected in 1960 with strong support from African American voters, made civil rights a top priority of his administration, urging Congress to enact meaningful legislation to address racial discrimination.

In 1963, following the Birmingham campaign and the March on Washington, Kennedy introduced a comprehensive civil rights bill aimed at ending segregation and discrimination in public accommodations, education, employment, and voting. The bill faced fierce opposition from Southern Democrats, who mounted filibusters and launched parliamentary maneuvers to derail its progress.

Despite these challenges, congressional leaders and civil rights advocates worked tirelessly to build bipartisan support for the bill. Senate Minority Leader Everett Dirksen, a Republican from Illinois, played a key role in rallying support among his colleagues and negotiating compromises to overcome Southern opposition.

Role of President Lyndon B. Johnson in Championing the Bill

Following President Kennedy's assassination in November 1963, Vice President Lyndon B. Johnson assumed the presidency and made the passage of the Civil Rights Act a top legislative priority. Drawing on his years of experience in Congress and his mastery of legislative politics, Johnson used his formidable powers of persuasion and arm-twisting to push the bill through Congress.

Johnson understood the importance of timing and strategy in navigating the legislative process. He skillfully exploited divisions within the Democratic Party and leveraged his personal relationships with lawmakers to secure their support for the bill. Johnson's famous "Johnson treatment," characterized by his persuasive charm, relentless lobbying, and occasional intimidation tactics, proved highly effective in winning over reluctant members of Congress.

Moreover, Johnson recognized the political calculus behind civil rights reform. He understood that the Democratic Party's future electoral prospects depended on its ability to attract African American voters and demonstrate its commitment to racial equality. By championing the Civil Rights Act, Johnson sought to solidify the Democratic Party's reputation as the party of civil rights and expand its coalition to include African Americans and liberal whites.

Throughout the legislative process, Johnson remained personally engaged in negotiations and decision-making, consulting with civil rights leaders, congressional allies, and administration officials to shape the bill's provisions and strategy. His leadership and determination were instrumental in overcoming the obstacles and opposition that threatened to derail the legislation.

Challenges and Compromises in Drafting the Legislation

Crafting the Civil Rights Act of 1964 required navigating a minefield of political, legal, and ideological obstacles. Lawmakers faced contentious debates over the scope and enforcement mechanisms of the bill, as well as fierce resistance from segregationist opponents determined to preserve the status quo.

One of the most contentious issues was the inclusion of Title II, which prohibited discrimination in public accommodations such as hotels, restaurants, theaters, and retail stores. Southern Democrats vehemently opposed this provision, arguing that it infringed upon states' rights and private property rights. In response, supporters of the bill sought to strike a delicate balance between protecting individual liberties and advancing the cause of racial equality.

Another key sticking point was the enforcement mechanism of the bill. Civil rights advocates pushed for robust federal enforcement powers to ensure compliance with the law and hold violators accountable. Southern opponents, however, feared federal overreach and sought to weaken the bill's enforcement provisions through amendments and filibusters.

In the face of these challenges, lawmakers engaged in a series of negotiations and compromises to reach consensus on the bill's final form. Key compromises included:

1. Exemption for Small Businesses: To address concerns about the impact of Title II on small businesses, lawmakers included exemptions for businesses with fewer than 15 employees, as well as limited exemptions for private clubs and religious organizations.

2. Weakening of Title VII: Title VII of the Civil Rights Act, which prohibited employment discrimination, initially included provisions for federal oversight of hiring practices and affirmative action measures. However, these provisions were watered down in response to opposition from conservative lawmakers, leading to compromises that weakened the bill's effectiveness in combating workplace discrimination.

3. Expansion of Federal Authority: Despite efforts to limit federal intervention, the final version of the Civil Rights Act granted broad powers to the federal government to enforce compliance with the law, including the authority to withhold federal funds from noncompliant states and institutions.

In the end, the Civil Rights Act of 1964 emerged as a carefully crafted compromise that sought to address the pressing need for racial equality while navigating the complexities of American politics and society. Its passage represented a historic victory for the Civil Rights Movement and a major step forward in the ongoing struggle for civil rights and social justice in America.

Chapter 5: Overview of the Civil Rights Act

The Civil Rights Act of 1964 stands as a monumental piece of legislation that aimed to dismantle racial discrimination and segregation in the United States. This chapter provides a detailed examination of the key provisions of the Civil Rights Act, highlighting the significance of each title and its impact on American society.

Title I: Voting Rights

Title I of the Civil Rights Act addressed the issue of voting rights, which had long been a primary target of segregationists seeking to disenfranchise African American voters. The provisions of Title I aimed to remove barriers to voting and ensure equal access to the ballot box for all citizens, regardless of race or color.

1. Prohibition of Discriminatory Voting Practices: Title I prohibited the use of literacy tests, poll taxes, and other discriminatory voting practices that had been used to disenfranchise African American voters in the South. These measures were designed to prevent eligible voters from exercising their constitutional right to vote and maintain white supremacy in the political arena.

2. Federal Oversight of Elections: Title I authorized the federal government to monitor and oversee elections in jurisdictions with a history of voter discrimination. The Attorney General was empowered to send federal examiners to register voters and ensure compliance with the law, particularly in states with a pattern of voter suppression tactics.

3. Expansion of Voter Registration: Title I sought to expand voter registration by removing barriers to participation and facilitating voter registration in communities with low turnout rates. It required states to provide assistance to individuals seeking to register to vote and mandated the availability of voter registration materials in multiple languages.

The provisions of Title I represented a significant step toward achieving equal voting rights for African Americans and other marginalized communities. By eliminating discriminatory voting practices and expanding access to the electoral process, Title I sought to strengthen democracy and promote political participation among all citizens.

Title II: Public Accommodations

Title II of the Civil Rights Act addressed the issue of racial segregation in public accommodations, such as hotels, restaurants, theaters, and retail stores. These establishments had long been sites of discrimination and exclusion, where African Americans were denied service or relegated to separate and inferior facilities.

1. Prohibition of Discrimination in Public Accommodations: Title II prohibited discrimination on the basis of race, color, religion, or national origin in public accommodations engaged in interstate commerce. It made it illegal to deny individuals access to public facilities or services based on their race or ethnicity, regardless of whether the establishment was privately owned.

2. Requirement for Equal Treatment: Title II mandated that all individuals be treated equally in places of public accommodation, without regard to their race or color. It prohibited segregation or separate treatment of patrons based on their race and required establishments to provide equal service, facilities, and accommodations to all customers.

3. Expansion of Federal Authority: Title II granted the federal government broad enforcement powers to ensure compliance with the law and investigate allegations of discrimination in public accommodations. It authorized the Attorney General to bring civil lawsuits against violators and seek injunctions to compel compliance with the law.

The provisions of Title II represented a significant departure from the era of Jim Crow segregation, where racial discrimination in public accommodations was commonplace and legally sanctioned. By outlawing segregation and discrimination in places of public accommodation, Title II sought to promote equality and ensure that all individuals could access essential services and facilities without fear of discrimination.

Title III: Desegregation of Public Facilities

Title III of the Civil Rights Act addressed the issue of racial segregation in public facilities and government-funded programs, such as parks, libraries, schools, and transportation systems. These facilities had long been segregated along racial lines, with African Americans denied equal access to essential services and amenities.

1. Prohibition of Segregation in Public Facilities: Title III prohibited racial segregation in any facility or service that was supported by federal funds or operated by a state or local government. It made it illegal to maintain separate facilities or services for individuals based on their race or color, regardless of whether the facility was publicly or privately owned.

2. Requirement for Equal Access: Title III mandated that all individuals have equal access to public facilities and services, without regard to their race or color. It prohibited the imposition of separate facilities or services for different racial groups and required government agencies to provide equal treatment and opportunities to all citizens.

3. Enforcement and Compliance: Title III authorized federal agencies to withhold funds from programs or facilities that practiced racial segregation or discrimination. It empowered the federal government to investigate complaints of segregation and take enforcement actions against violators, including the termination of federal funding for noncompliant entities.

The provisions of Title III aimed to dismantle the infrastructure of segregation that had long divided communities along racial lines. By outlawing segregation in public facilities and government programs, Title III sought to create more inclusive and equitable spaces where all individuals could access essential services and amenities without regard to their race or color.

Title IV: Desegregation of Public Education

Title IV of the Civil Rights Act addressed the issue of racial segregation in public education, which had been a central battleground in the fight for civil rights since the landmark Supreme Court decision in Brown v. Board of Education (1954). Despite the Court's ruling, many schools remained segregated, perpetuating inequality and denying African American students equal educational opportunities.

1. Prohibition of Racial Segregation in Schools: Title IV prohibited racial segregation in public schools and other educational institutions that received federal funding. It made it illegal to maintain separate schools or educational

programs for students based on their race or color and required the desegregation of all public schools.

2. Requirement for Integration: Title IV mandated that all public schools adopt policies and practices to promote racial integration and ensure equal educational opportunities for all students. It prohibited the use of race-based criteria for student assignment, faculty hiring, or educational resources allocation and required schools to take affirmative steps to overcome the effects of past discrimination.

3. Enforcement and Compliance: Title IV empowered the federal government to withhold funds from school districts that failed to comply with desegregation orders or implement integration measures. It authorized the Department of Education to investigate complaints of racial segregation in schools and take enforcement actions against noncompliant districts.

The provisions of Title IV represented a significant escalation in the federal government's efforts to desegregate public schools and ensure equal educational opportunities for all students. By outlawing racial segregation and mandating integration, Title IV sought to dismantle the legacy of Jim Crow education and create more inclusive and equitable learning environments for children of all races.

Title V: Commission on Civil Rights

Title V of the Civil Rights Act established the United States Commission on Civil Rights, an independent federal agency tasked with investigating and monitoring civil rights violations. The commission was charged with documenting instances of discrimination and recommending policy changes to address systemic injustices.

1. Creation of the Commission: Title V created the United States Commission on Civil Rights, consisting of eight members appointed by the President and confirmed by the Senate. The commission was tasked with conducting investigations, holding hearings, and issuing reports on civil rights issues affecting the nation.

2. Powers and Responsibilities: The Commission on Civil Rights was granted broad authority to investigate allegations of discrimination in voting rights, employment, housing, education, and other areas. It had the power to

subpoena witnesses, compel the production of evidence, and hold public hearings to gather information on civil rights violations.

3. Reporting and Recommendations: The commission was required to submit annual reports to the President and Congress detailing its findings and recommendations for addressing civil rights issues. These reports served as a critical source of information for policymakers, lawmakers, and advocates seeking to address systemic injustices and promote equality.

The establishment of the Commission on Civil Rights represented a significant commitment by the federal government to address racial discrimination and promote civil rights at the national level. By providing a platform for investigating and documenting civil rights violations, the commission played a crucial role in shaping public policy and advancing the cause of racial equality in America.

In summary, the Civil Rights Act of 1964 comprised five key titles, each addressing different aspects of racial discrimination and segregation in American society. From voting rights and public accommodations to desegregation in education and public facilities, the provisions of the Civil Rights Act sought to dismantle the legal framework of segregation and promote equality and justice for all citizens. By examining the key provisions of the act, we gain a deeper understanding of its significance as a milestone in the ongoing struggle for civil rights and social justice in America.

Chapter 6: Grassroots Activism

Grassroots activism played a pivotal role in the Civil Rights Movement, mobilizing ordinary citizens across the country to demand an end to racial discrimination and segregation. This chapter explores the crucial role of grassroots movements and protests in pushing for civil rights legislation, highlighting the contributions of key activists such as Martin Luther King Jr., Rosa Parks, and others, and examining the impact of nonviolent resistance tactics in effecting social change.

Role of Grassroots Movements and Protests

Grassroots movements were the backbone of the Civil Rights Movement, providing the energy, momentum, and grassroots support necessary to challenge entrenched systems of racial oppression. From local organizing efforts to mass demonstrations and boycotts, grassroots activists employed a variety of tactics to mobilize communities, raise awareness, and demand justice.

1. Local Organizing: Grassroots activists worked tirelessly to organize local communities and build networks of support for civil rights initiatives. Through churches, community centers, and neighborhood associations, activists engaged in door-to-door canvassing, voter registration drives, and educational campaigns to empower citizens and mobilize support for civil rights causes.

2. Mass Demonstrations: Mass demonstrations and protests served as powerful tools for raising awareness and putting pressure on policymakers to enact civil rights legislation. Events such as the March on Washington for Jobs and Freedom (1963), the Selma to Montgomery marches (1965), and the Birmingham campaign (1963) drew national attention to the plight of African Americans and galvanized support for civil rights reform.

3. Boycotts and Economic Pressure: Grassroots activists organized boycotts and economic pressure campaigns to challenge segregation and discrimination in local businesses and industries. The Montgomery Bus Boycott (1955-1956), sparked by Rosa Parks' refusal to give up her seat on a segregated bus, demonstrated the economic power of African American consumers and forced policymakers to reconsider discriminatory practices.

4. Student Activism: Students played a significant role in the Civil Rights Movement, organizing sit-ins, marches, and demonstrations to protest segregation and demand equal rights. Student-led organizations such as the Student Nonviolent Coordinating Committee (SNCC) and the Congress of Racial Equality (CORE) mobilized young activists and provided leadership and resources for grassroots organizing efforts.

5. Legal Advocacy: Grassroots activists engaged in legal advocacy to challenge segregation and discrimination in the courts. Organizations such as the NAACP Legal Defense Fund, led by Thurgood Marshall, pursued litigation strategies to challenge Jim Crow laws and secure landmark victories in cases such as Brown v. Board of Education (1954) and Heart of Atlanta Motel v. United States (1964).

Through their collective action and determination, grassroots activists helped to shift public opinion, raise awareness of civil rights issues, and create pressure for legislative change. Their efforts laid the groundwork for the passage of the Civil Rights Act of 1964 and subsequent civil rights legislation, leaving a lasting legacy of social justice and equality.

Contributions of Activists

Several key activists played instrumental roles in the grassroots activism of the Civil Rights Movement, contributing their leadership, courage, and sacrifice to the struggle for racial equality. Among the most prominent were:

1. Martin Luther King Jr.: Reverend Martin Luther King Jr. emerged as the preeminent leader of the Civil Rights Movement, advocating for nonviolent resistance and civil disobedience as powerful tools for social change. King's leadership during the Montgomery Bus Boycott, the Birmingham campaign, and the March on Washington helped to galvanize support for civil rights reform and inspire millions of Americans to join the fight for justice.

2. Rosa Parks: Rosa Parks' act of defiance on a segregated bus in Montgomery, Alabama, sparked the Montgomery Bus Boycott and symbolized the power of individual resistance in the face of injustice. Parks' quiet courage and refusal to accept segregation galvanized the African American community and laid the foundation for the Civil Rights Movement.

3. John Lewis: John Lewis, a leader of the Student Nonviolent Coordinating Committee (SNCC) and a key organizer of the Selma to Montgomery marches, was instrumental in mobilizing young activists and organizing nonviolent protests against segregation and voter suppression. Lewis' commitment to nonviolent resistance and his willingness to endure violence and imprisonment for the cause of civil rights inspired a new generation of activists.

4. Ella Baker: As a grassroots organizer and strategist, Ella Baker played a crucial role in empowering local communities and fostering leadership among ordinary citizens. Baker's work with organizations such as the Southern Christian Leadership Conference (SCLC) and the Student Nonviolent Coordinating Committee (SNCC) helped to mobilize grassroots support for civil rights initiatives and amplify the voices of marginalized communities.

5. Fannie Lou Hamer: Fannie Lou Hamer, a sharecropper and voting rights activist from Mississippi, became a powerful voice for African American rights and political empowerment. Hamer's impassioned speeches, fearless advocacy, and tireless organizing efforts helped to mobilize African American voters and challenge the entrenched systems of racial discrimination and voter suppression in the South.

These activists, along with countless others, played critical roles in the grassroots activism of the Civil Rights Movement, demonstrating courage, resilience, and determination in the face of overwhelming odds. Their contributions helped to mobilize communities, raise awareness, and push for legislative change, laying the groundwork for the passage of the Civil Rights Act of 1964 and the broader struggle for racial equality in America.

Impact of Nonviolent Resistance Tactics

Nonviolent resistance tactics were central to the success of the Civil Rights Movement, providing a powerful means of challenging injustice and mobilizing support for civil rights reform. Inspired by the teachings of Mahatma Gandhi and the principles of Christian love and forgiveness, nonviolent resistance became a defining characteristic of the movement and a source of moral authority and legitimacy.

1. Moral High Ground: Nonviolent resistance tactics allowed civil rights activists to claim the moral high ground and appeal to the conscience of the

nation. By refusing to respond to violence with violence, activists demonstrated their commitment to justice and righteousness and exposed the brutality and injustice of segregationist policies.

2. Strategic Disruption: Nonviolent resistance tactics such as sit-ins, marches, and boycotts were strategically designed to disrupt the status quo and draw attention to the injustices of segregation and discrimination. By occupying public spaces, blocking traffic, and disrupting business as usual, activists forced policymakers and the public to confront the reality of racial inequality.

3. Media Attention: Nonviolent protests generated widespread media coverage and drew national and international attention to the Civil Rights Movement. Images of peaceful demonstrators being beaten by police, attacked by dogs, and hosed down with fire hoses shocked the conscience of the nation and galvanized support for civil rights reform.

4. Building Coalitions: Nonviolent resistance tactics helped to build coalitions and alliances across racial, religious, and ideological lines. By appealing to the shared values of justice, equality, and human dignity, civil rights activists were able to mobilize support from diverse communities and create a broad-based movement for social change.

5. Empowerment of Communities: Nonviolent resistance empowered ordinary citizens to take action and challenge injustice in their own communities. Through acts of civil disobedience, protest, and collective action, grassroots activists demonstrated that individuals had the power to effect change and hold their leaders accountable for their actions.

The impact of nonviolent resistance tactics extended far beyond the immediate goals of the Civil Rights Movement, inspiring movements for social justice and liberation around the world. By demonstrating the power of love, courage, and collective action, civil rights activists paved the way for a more inclusive, equitable, and compassionate society.

In conclusion, grassroots activism was instrumental in pushing for civil rights legislation and effecting social change during the Civil Rights Movement. Through local organizing, mass demonstrations, and nonviolent resistance tactics, activists mobilized communities, raised awareness, and challenged the entrenched systems of racial discrimination and segregation. Their contributions, along with the leadership of figures such as Martin Luther King Jr. and Rosa

Parks, helped to galvanize support for civil rights reform and lay the foundation for a more just and equitable society.

Chapter 7: Legal Challenges and Supreme Court Decisions

The Civil Rights Act of 1964 represented a monumental achievement in the fight for racial equality in the United States. However, its passage did not mark the end of the struggle. In the years that followed, the act faced numerous legal challenges, and its provisions were subject to interpretation and enforcement by the judicial branch. This chapter explores the legal challenges to the Civil Rights Act, landmark Supreme Court decisions interpreting and upholding the act, and the significance of these court rulings in shaping civil rights enforcement in America.

Legal Challenges to the Civil Rights Act

Almost immediately after its passage, the Civil Rights Act of 1964 faced legal challenges from opponents seeking to undermine its effectiveness and restrict its scope. These challenges came in various forms, including lawsuits brought by individuals, businesses, and state governments, as well as efforts by Congress to amend or weaken the act through legislative means.

1. Constitutional Challenges: One of the primary legal challenges to the Civil Rights Act was based on constitutional grounds, particularly the Commerce Clause and the Fourteenth Amendment. Opponents argued that Congress had exceeded its authority under the Commerce Clause by regulating private businesses engaged in intrastate commerce. They also contended that certain provisions of the act, such as Title II's prohibition of discrimination in public accommodations, violated the Fourteenth Amendment's guarantee of equal protection under the law.

2. State Resistance: In several Southern states, officials openly defied the provisions of the Civil Rights Act and refused to comply with federal desegregation orders. State governments passed laws and ordinances aimed at circumventing the act's requirements, leading to legal battles and federal intervention to enforce compliance.

3. Legal Loopholes and Evasion: Some opponents of the Civil Rights Act sought to exploit legal loopholes and evade its provisions through creative legal

maneuvers. For example, businesses and institutions attempted to circumvent the prohibition of racial discrimination in public accommodations by claiming exemptions for private clubs or religious organizations.

Despite these legal challenges, the Civil Rights Act withstood scrutiny and remained the law of the land, thanks in part to landmark Supreme Court decisions that upheld its constitutionality and affirmed the federal government's authority to combat racial discrimination and segregation.

Landmark Supreme Court Decisions Interpreting and Upholding the Act

The Supreme Court played a crucial role in interpreting and upholding the Civil Rights Act of 1964, issuing several landmark decisions that clarified the scope of the act and affirmed its constitutionality. These decisions established important legal precedents and expanded the protections afforded by the act to encompass a broader range of civil rights issues.

1. Heart of Atlanta Motel v. United States (1964): In this landmark case, the Supreme Court upheld the constitutionality of Title II of the Civil Rights Act, which prohibited racial discrimination in public accommodations engaged in interstate commerce. The Court ruled that Congress had the authority under the Commerce Clause to regulate private businesses that served interstate travelers and that racial discrimination in public accommodations constituted an unconstitutional burden on interstate commerce.

2. Katzenbach v. McClung (1964): In another pivotal case, the Supreme Court upheld the constitutionality of Title II of the Civil Rights Act in the context of a restaurant's refusal to serve African American customers. The Court held that Congress had the authority to regulate discriminatory practices that had a substantial effect on interstate commerce, even if the business in question primarily served local customers.

3. Jones v. Alfred H. Mayer Co. (1968): This Supreme Court decision expanded the protections of the Civil Rights Act to encompass private acts of racial discrimination in housing. The Court held that the act prohibited racial discrimination in the sale or rental of housing, even if the discrimination was perpetrated by private individuals or entities rather than state actors.

4. Griggs v. Duke Power Co. (1971): In this case, the Supreme Court addressed the issue of employment discrimination and disparate impact under Title VII of the Civil Rights Act. The Court ruled that employers could be held liable for practices that had a disparate impact on protected groups, even if the practices were not explicitly discriminatory, and that employers bore the burden of proving that such practices were job-related and consistent with business necessity.

These landmark Supreme Court decisions affirmed the constitutionality of the Civil Rights Act and expanded its protections to encompass a broader range of civil rights issues, including racial discrimination in public accommodations, housing, and employment. They provided important legal precedents for future civil rights litigation and enforcement efforts and reaffirmed the federal government's authority to combat racial discrimination and promote equality under the law.

Significance of Court Rulings in Shaping Civil Rights Enforcement

The Supreme Court's rulings interpreting and upholding the Civil Rights Act had far-reaching implications for civil rights enforcement in America. By affirming the constitutionality of the act and expanding its protections to cover new areas of civil rights violations, the Court played a critical role in shaping the trajectory of the Civil Rights Movement and advancing the cause of racial equality.

1. Legal Precedents: The Supreme Court's decisions established important legal precedents that clarified the scope and interpretation of the Civil Rights Act. These precedents provided guidance for lower courts and future litigants in navigating complex civil rights issues and resolving disputes over the act's enforcement and application.

2. Expanded Protections: The Court's rulings expanded the protections afforded by the Civil Rights Act to encompass a broader range of civil rights violations, including racial discrimination in housing, employment, and public accommodations. This expansion of protections helped to address systemic injustices and provide recourse for individuals and communities affected by discrimination.

3. Federal Authority: The Court's decisions reaffirmed the federal government's authority to combat racial discrimination and enforce civil rights laws. By upholding the constitutionality of the act and affirming Congress's power to regulate interstate commerce and protect civil rights, the Court bolstered the federal government's role as a guardian of civil rights and equal justice under the law.

4. Social Change: The Supreme Court's rulings had a profound impact on social attitudes and norms regarding race and equality. By condemning racial discrimination as unconstitutional and affirming the principle of equal protection under the law, the Court helped to shift public opinion and promote a more inclusive and equitable society.

In summary, the Supreme Court's decisions interpreting and upholding the Civil Rights Act of 1964 played a crucial role in shaping civil rights enforcement in America. By affirming the constitutionality of the act, expanding its protections, and reaffirming the federal government's authority to combat racial discrimination, the Court helped to advance the cause of racial equality and justice for all citizens. These landmark decisions provided important legal precedents and set the stage for future civil rights litigation and enforcement efforts, leaving a lasting legacy of progress and social change.

Chapter 8: Implementation and Enforcement

The passage of the Civil Rights Act of 1964 marked a historic milestone in the struggle for racial equality in the United States. However, the effectiveness of the act depended not only on its passage but also on its implementation and enforcement at the state and local levels. This chapter examines the challenges in implementing the Civil Rights Act, the establishment of federal agencies to enforce civil rights laws, and the impact of civil rights enforcement actions on communities across the country.

Challenges in Implementing the Civil Rights Act at the State and Local Levels

Implementing the Civil Rights Act at the state and local levels posed significant challenges, as entrenched systems of racial discrimination and segregation continued to resist change. Despite the legal mandate provided by the act, many states and localities were slow to comply with its provisions and resisted efforts to desegregate public facilities, schools, and workplaces. Several factors contributed to these challenges:

1. Resistance from Segregationist Officials: In many Southern states, segregationist officials openly defied federal desegregation orders and refused to comply with the provisions of the Civil Rights Act. State governments passed laws and ordinances aimed at circumventing the act's requirements, leading to legal battles and federal intervention to enforce compliance.

2. Lack of Political Will: In some cases, state and local officials lacked the political will or resources to enforce the Civil Rights Act effectively. Despite federal mandates, some jurisdictions failed to allocate sufficient funding or personnel to implement desegregation measures or ensure compliance with antidiscrimination laws.

3. Social Resistance and Backlash: Implementation of the Civil Rights Act faced resistance and backlash from segments of the white community opposed to racial integration and equality. Segregationist groups organized protests, boycotts, and acts of violence to intimidate African Americans and disrupt desegregation efforts, creating a climate of fear and uncertainty.

4. Legal Maneuvering and Delay Tactics: Opponents of civil rights reform employed legal maneuvering and delay tactics to frustrate efforts to implement and enforce the Civil Rights Act. Lawsuits, appeals, and administrative challenges were used to tie up desegregation orders in court and delay compliance with federal mandates.

Despite these challenges, civil rights activists and federal officials worked tirelessly to overcome resistance and ensure the effective implementation of the Civil Rights Act. Through litigation, advocacy, and grassroots organizing, they sought to hold state and local governments accountable for their obligations under the law and promote racial equality and justice for all citizens.

Establishment of Federal Agencies to Enforce Civil Rights Laws

To enforce the provisions of the Civil Rights Act and combat racial discrimination and segregation, the federal government established several agencies tasked with investigating complaints, enforcing antidiscrimination laws, and promoting equal opportunity. These agencies played a crucial role in monitoring compliance with the act and holding violators accountable for their actions:

1. Equal Employment Opportunity Commission (EEOC): The EEOC was created to enforce Title VII of the Civil Rights Act, which prohibits employment discrimination on the basis of race, color, religion, sex, or national origin. The EEOC investigates complaints of discrimination, conducts hearings and investigations, and litigates cases of employment discrimination on behalf of aggrieved individuals.

2. Office for Civil Rights (OCR): The OCR, housed within the Department of Education, is responsible for enforcing Title VI of the Civil Rights Act, which prohibits discrimination on the basis of race, color, or national origin in federally funded education programs and activities. The OCR investigates complaints of discrimination, conducts compliance reviews, and works with educational institutions to ensure compliance with civil rights laws.

3. Civil Rights Division of the Department of Justice (DOJ): The Civil Rights Division of the DOJ is responsible for enforcing federal civil rights laws, including the Civil Rights Act of 1964. The division investigates and litigates

cases of discrimination in areas such as voting rights, housing, education, and public accommodations, and works to protect the rights of individuals and communities facing discrimination.

4. Department of Housing and Urban Development (HUD): HUD is responsible for enforcing the Fair Housing Act, which prohibits discrimination in housing on the basis of race, color, religion, sex, familial status, national origin, or disability. HUD investigates complaints of housing discrimination, conducts fair housing testing, and works to promote fair and inclusive housing practices.

These federal agencies played a critical role in enforcing civil rights laws and promoting equal opportunity and access to essential services and opportunities. Through their enforcement actions, investigations, and outreach efforts, they sought to combat discrimination and promote a more inclusive and equitable society for all Americans.

Civil Rights Enforcement Actions and Their Impact on Communities

Civil rights enforcement actions had a profound impact on communities across the country, shaping the landscape of racial equality and social justice. By investigating complaints, litigating cases, and holding violators accountable for their actions, federal agencies sought to address systemic injustices and promote equal opportunity and access to essential services. Several key areas of civil rights enforcement and their impact on communities include:

1. Desegregation of Schools: Civil rights enforcement actions led to the desegregation of public schools and the dismantling of racially segregated education systems. Through litigation and court orders, federal agencies worked to ensure that all students had equal access to quality education and educational opportunities, regardless of their race or ethnicity.

2. Employment Discrimination: Federal agencies investigated complaints of employment discrimination and worked to hold employers accountable for discriminatory practices. By promoting equal employment opportunities and combating workplace discrimination, civil rights enforcement actions helped to create more inclusive and diverse workplaces and expand economic opportunities for minorities and women.

3. Access to Public Accommodations: Civil rights enforcement actions targeted discrimination in public accommodations such as hotels, restaurants, theaters, and retail stores. By investigating complaints and litigating cases of discrimination, federal agencies sought to ensure that all individuals had equal access to essential services and facilities, regardless of their race or ethnicity.

4. Voting Rights: Civil rights enforcement actions aimed to protect and expand access to the ballot box and combat voter suppression tactics. By investigating complaints of voter discrimination and challenging restrictive voting laws, federal agencies worked to safeguard the right to vote and promote greater political participation among minority and marginalized communities.

5. Fair Housing Practices: Federal agencies worked to combat housing discrimination and promote fair and inclusive housing practices. Through investigations, fair housing testing, and enforcement actions, they sought to ensure that all individuals had equal access to housing opportunities and were protected from discrimination in the housing market.

Overall, civil rights enforcement actions played a critical role in advancing the cause of racial equality and social justice in America. By addressing systemic injustices, promoting equal opportunity, and holding violators accountable for their actions, federal agencies helped to create a more inclusive and equitable society for all Americans. While challenges remained, the legacy of civil rights enforcement continues to shape the landscape of civil rights and social justice in the United States today.

Chapter 9: Immediate Effects and Reactions

The passage of the Civil Rights Act of 1964 had a profound and immediate impact on American society, sparking reactions from both supporters and opponents of the legislation. This chapter explores the immediate effects of the Civil Rights Act on American society, the reactions it elicited from various quarters, and the social and cultural shifts resulting from its passage.

Immediate Effects of the Civil Rights Act on American Society

The Civil Rights Act of 1964 ushered in a new era of civil rights and equality in America, with several immediate effects on society:

1. Desegregation of Public Facilities: One of the most visible and immediate effects of the Civil Rights Act was the desegregation of public facilities such as restaurants, hotels, theaters, and parks. The act prohibited racial discrimination in places of public accommodation engaged in interstate commerce, leading to the integration of previously segregated spaces.

2. Expansion of Voting Rights: The Voting Rights Act of 1965, a companion piece of legislation to the Civil Rights Act, expanded access to the ballot box for African Americans by removing barriers to voter registration and outlawing discriminatory voting practices. The act led to a significant increase in African American voter registration and political participation.

3. End of Legal Segregation: The Civil Rights Act effectively ended legal segregation in the United States by outlawing discriminatory practices and policies based on race, color, religion, sex, or national origin. It paved the way for the dismantling of Jim Crow laws and the abolition of racial segregation in public schools, workplaces, and other institutions.

4. Empowerment of Minority Communities: The Civil Rights Act empowered minority communities to assert their rights and demand equal treatment under the law. African Americans, in particular, gained a newfound sense of agency and self-determination, challenging systemic injustices and advocating for social and political change.

5. Shift in Social Attitudes: The Civil Rights Act precipitated a shift in social attitudes and norms regarding race, equality, and justice. It challenged deeply ingrained beliefs and prejudices about racial superiority and inferiority and forced Americans to confront the reality of systemic racism and discrimination.

Reactions from Supporters and Opponents of the Legislation

The Civil Rights Act elicited a range of reactions from supporters and opponents of the legislation, reflecting deep divisions within American society:

1. Supporters: Supporters of the Civil Rights Act hailed its passage as a long overdue victory for justice and equality. Civil rights activists, religious leaders, labor unions, and progressive lawmakers celebrated the act as a significant step toward ending racial discrimination and achieving full civil rights for all Americans.

2. Opponents: Opponents of the Civil Rights Act viewed it as an infringement on states' rights and individual freedoms. Segregationists, conservative lawmakers, and white supremacist groups decried the act as government overreach and resisted its implementation through legal challenges, protests, and acts of defiance.

3. Mixed Reactions: Many Americans held ambivalent or mixed views on the Civil Rights Act, torn between their commitment to equality and their fears of social upheaval and change. Some supported the goals of the act but questioned its methods or timing, while others opposed the act outright but grudgingly accepted its provisions in the face of federal enforcement.

4. International Response: The passage of the Civil Rights Act also garnered international attention, with many countries applauding America's efforts to address racial discrimination and uphold human rights. The act served as a beacon of hope and inspiration for oppressed peoples around the world, fueling aspirations for freedom and equality in other nations.

Social and Cultural Shifts Resulting from the Act's Passage

The Civil Rights Act precipitated profound social and cultural shifts in American society, reshaping the nation's identity and values in fundamental ways:

1. Integration and Diversity: The act fostered greater integration and diversity in American society by breaking down barriers to racial segregation and discrimination. It paved the way for the emergence of more inclusive and multicultural communities, where individuals of different races, ethnicities, and backgrounds could live and work together in harmony.

2. Empowerment of Minorities: The Civil Rights Act empowered minority communities to assert their rights and claim their rightful place in American society. African Americans, in particular, gained access to previously closed doors of opportunity in education, employment, and politics, laying the foundation for a new generation of leaders and activists.

3. Reckoning with Racism: The Civil Rights Act forced Americans to confront the legacy of racism and discrimination in their midst. It prompted soul-searching and reflection on the part of individuals and institutions, challenging them to acknowledge and address the injustices of the past and work toward a more equitable future.

4. Legacy of Activism: The passage of the Civil Rights Act inspired a new wave of activism and social change, fueling movements for women's rights, LGBTQ+ rights, disability rights, and other forms of social justice. It demonstrated the power of collective action and grassroots organizing in effecting meaningful and lasting change in society.

In conclusion, the Civil Rights Act of 1964 had a profound and immediate impact on American society, sparking reactions from both supporters and opponents of the legislation. It ushered in a new era of civil rights and equality, dismantling legal segregation and discrimination and empowering minority communities to assert their rights and demand equal treatment under the law. The act precipitated social and cultural shifts that reshaped the nation's identity and values, fostering greater integration, diversity, and empowerment in American society. Its legacy continues to reverberate today, reminding us of the ongoing struggle for justice and equality in America and inspiring future generations to continue the fight for civil rights and social justice.

Chapter 10: Legacy of the Civil Rights Act

The Civil Rights Act of 1964 stands as a cornerstone of American law and a beacon of hope for equality and justice. Its long-term impact on American society extends far beyond its immediate effects, shaping the trajectory of civil rights legislation, movements, and struggles for racial equality. This chapter explores the enduring legacy of the Civil Rights Act, its profound impact on American law and society, subsequent civil rights legislation and movements, and the continued struggles for racial equality in the United States.

Long-Term Impact of the Civil Rights Act on American Law and Society

The Civil Rights Act of 1964 fundamentally transformed American law and society, leaving a lasting legacy of progress and change:

1. Legal Protections: The act established important legal protections against discrimination on the basis of race, color, religion, sex, or national origin, laying the groundwork for future civil rights legislation and judicial decisions. It provided a framework for combating systemic injustice and promoting equality under the law.

2. Expansion of Civil Rights: The Civil Rights Act expanded the scope of civil rights protections in America, addressing not only racial discrimination but also discrimination based on religion, sex, and national origin. It set a precedent for future civil rights legislation aimed at protecting the rights of marginalized and vulnerable groups.

3. Enforcement Mechanisms: The act created federal agencies and enforcement mechanisms to ensure compliance with its provisions, empowering the federal government to investigate complaints of discrimination, litigate cases, and enforce civil rights laws. These enforcement mechanisms helped to hold violators accountable for their actions and promote greater accountability and transparency in civil rights enforcement.

4. Cultural Shifts: The Civil Rights Act precipitated profound cultural shifts in American society, challenging prevailing attitudes and norms regarding race, equality, and justice. It forced Americans to confront the legacy of racism and

discrimination in their midst and inspired a new wave of activism and social change.

5. Legacy of Activism: The Civil Rights Act inspired a new generation of activists and leaders to continue the fight for racial equality and social justice. It demonstrated the power of collective action and grassroots organizing in effecting meaningful and lasting change in society, laying the foundation for future civil rights movements and struggles.

Subsequent Civil Rights Legislation and Movements

The Civil Rights Act of 1964 served as a catalyst for subsequent civil rights legislation and movements, expanding the scope of civil rights protections and advancing the cause of racial equality:

1. Voting Rights Act of 1965: Building on the momentum of the Civil Rights Act, Congress passed the Voting Rights Act of 1965, which aimed to address racial discrimination in voting and ensure greater access to the ballot box for African Americans and other minority groups. The act prohibited discriminatory voting practices such as literacy tests and poll taxes and authorized federal oversight of election procedures in states with a history of voter suppression.

2. Fair Housing Act of 1968: The Fair Housing Act of 1968, also known as the Civil Rights Act of 1968, expanded civil rights protections to encompass housing discrimination based on race, color, religion, sex, familial status, or national origin. The act prohibited discrimination in the sale, rental, and financing of housing and provided enforcement mechanisms to address violations of fair housing laws.

3. Affirmative Action Policies: In the decades following the Civil Rights Act, policymakers implemented affirmative action policies aimed at promoting diversity and equal opportunity in education, employment, and government contracting. These policies sought to address historical patterns of discrimination and promote greater representation and inclusion of minority groups in all sectors of society.

4. Women's Rights Movement: The Civil Rights Act provided inspiration and momentum for the women's rights movement, which sought to address gender discrimination and promote equal rights and opportunities for women.

Women activists mobilized around issues such as reproductive rights, workplace equality, and gender-based violence, leading to significant legal and social reforms in the decades that followed.

5. LGBTQ+ Rights Movement: The Civil Rights Act also provided a foundation for the LGBTQ+ rights movement, which sought to address discrimination and promote equal rights and protections for LGBTQ+ individuals. Activists mobilized around issues such as marriage equality, nondiscrimination protections, and LGBTQ+ rights in the workplace, leading to landmark legal victories and social change.

Continued Struggles for Racial Equality in the United States

Despite the progress made since the passage of the Civil Rights Act, the struggle for racial equality in the United States continues to this day:

1. Persistent Racial Disparities: Racial disparities persist in areas such as education, employment, healthcare, housing, and criminal justice, reflecting ongoing systemic inequalities and barriers to opportunity for minority communities.

2. Police Brutality and Racial Profiling: Incidents of police brutality and racial profiling continue to occur, sparking protests and calls for police reform and accountability. Communities of color disproportionately bear the brunt of discriminatory policing practices and systemic racism within the criminal justice system.

3. Voter Suppression and Disenfranchisement: Efforts to restrict voting rights and suppress minority voter turnout remain a significant challenge to democracy. Voter suppression tactics such as voter ID laws, gerrymandering, and purges of voter rolls disproportionately affect minority communities and undermine the principle of equal access to the ballot box.

4. Economic Inequality: Economic inequality persists along racial lines, with minority communities facing higher rates of poverty, unemployment, and economic insecurity. Structural barriers to economic opportunity, such as lack of access to quality education, affordable housing, and financial resources, perpetuate cycles of poverty and disadvantage.

5. Educational Disparities: Racial disparities in education continue to hinder opportunities for minority students, with unequal access to resources, high-quality schools, and opportunities for academic achievement. Segregation and funding disparities exacerbate educational inequities and contribute to persistent achievement gaps between racial and ethnic groups.

In conclusion, the Civil Rights Act of 1964 left a profound and enduring legacy on American law and society, shaping the trajectory of civil rights legislation, movements, and struggles for racial equality. Its long-term impact can be seen in the expansion of civil rights protections, the advancement of minority rights and opportunities, and the ongoing fight for justice and equality in America. While progress has been made, challenges remain in addressing systemic racism and achieving true racial equity and inclusion. The legacy of the Civil Rights Act reminds us of the ongoing struggle for racial equality and the importance of continuing to work towards a more just and equitable society for all.

Chapter 11: International Influence

The Civil Rights Act of 1964 reverberated far beyond the borders of the United States, leaving an indelible mark on global human rights movements and shaping international norms of equality and justice. This chapter explores the influence of the Civil Rights Act on global human rights movements, international reactions and responses to its passage, and the enduring legacy of the act in shaping international norms of equality and justice.

Influence of the Civil Rights Act on Global Human Rights Movements

The Civil Rights Act of 1964 served as a catalyst for human rights movements around the world, inspiring oppressed peoples to demand justice, equality, and dignity. Its principles of non-discrimination, equal protection under the law, and the right to freedom from racial discrimination resonated with individuals and communities facing similar struggles for liberation and human rights. The influence of the Civil Rights Act on global human rights movements can be seen in several key ways:

1. Inspiration for Liberation Movements: The Civil Rights Act inspired liberation movements in Africa, Asia, Latin America, and beyond, providing a powerful example of collective action and resistance against oppression. Movements for decolonization, indigenous rights, and self-determination drew inspiration from the civil rights struggle in the United States, adapting its tactics and strategies to their own contexts.

2. Solidarity and Internationalism: The civil rights movement in the United States forged connections with liberation movements around the world, fostering a sense of solidarity and internationalism among oppressed peoples. Civil rights leaders such as Martin Luther King Jr. and Malcolm X spoke out against colonialism, imperialism, and apartheid, highlighting the interconnectedness of struggles for justice and freedom.

3. Legal Precedents and International Law: The Civil Rights Act contributed to the development of international human rights law and norms, serving as a model for anti-discrimination legislation in other countries and influencing

the adoption of international human rights treaties. Its provisions on non-discrimination and equal protection under the law helped to shape the jurisprudence of international human rights bodies and tribunals.

4. Global Impact of Nonviolent Resistance: The civil rights movement in the United States popularized the use of nonviolent resistance as a powerful tool for social change, inspiring movements for peace, democracy, and human rights around the world. The tactics of sit-ins, boycotts, and marches employed by civil rights activists became emblematic of grassroots mobilization and resistance against injustice.

International Reactions and Responses to the Act's Passage

The passage of the Civil Rights Act elicited a range of reactions and responses from the international community, reflecting the global significance of the legislation and its impact on international perceptions of the United States:

1. Celebration and Support: Many countries and international organizations celebrated the passage of the Civil Rights Act as a historic milestone in the struggle for racial equality and human rights. Governments, civil society organizations, and individuals around the world expressed solidarity with the civil rights movement and its goals of justice, freedom, and equality for all.

2. Criticism of Hypocrisy and Double Standards: Despite the passage of the Civil Rights Act, the United States faced criticism from some quarters for its perceived hypocrisy and double standards in promoting human rights abroad while failing to fully address racial discrimination and inequality at home. Critics pointed to ongoing segregation, police brutality, and systemic racism as evidence of America's unfinished business on civil rights.

3. Global Anti-Apartheid Movement: The Civil Rights Act galvanized the global anti-apartheid movement, which sought to dismantle the system of racial segregation and discrimination in South Africa. Civil rights activists in the United States played a key role in supporting the struggle against apartheid, advocating for economic sanctions, divestment, and international pressure to isolate the apartheid regime.

4. Influence on International Human Rights Law: The Civil Rights Act influenced the development of international human rights law and norms,

particularly in the areas of non-discrimination, equal protection under the law, and the right to freedom from racial discrimination. Its passage helped to elevate racial equality to the forefront of the international human rights agenda and provided inspiration for anti-discrimination efforts worldwide.

Legacy of the Act in Shaping International Norms of Equality and Justice

The legacy of the Civil Rights Act continues to shape international norms of equality and justice, inspiring movements for human rights and social justice around the world:

1. Promotion of Equality and Non-Discrimination: The Civil Rights Act advanced the principles of equality and non-discrimination as fundamental human rights, influencing international efforts to combat racism, discrimination, and inequality in all its forms. Its passage helped to elevate racial equality to the status of a universal human rights norm and provided a model for anti-discrimination legislation worldwide.

2. Advancement of Civil Rights Diplomacy: The Civil Rights Act bolstered America's credibility and influence in promoting civil rights and democracy abroad, serving as a cornerstone of civil rights diplomacy and foreign policy. The United States used its commitment to civil rights as a tool for diplomacy, advocating for human rights, democracy, and the rule of law on the global stage.

3. Inspiration for Social Movements: The Civil Rights Act inspired social movements for justice and equality in countries around the world, including movements for indigenous rights, women's rights, LGBTQ+ rights, and disability rights. Its legacy lives on in the struggles of oppressed peoples everywhere who seek to dismantle systems of oppression and achieve full recognition of their human rights.

4. Call to Action Against Racism and Injustice: The Civil Rights Act serves as a call to action against racism, injustice, and inequality wherever they exist. Its legacy reminds us of the ongoing struggle for racial equality and the importance of standing up for human rights and dignity for all people, regardless of race, ethnicity, religion, gender, or nationality.

In conclusion, the Civil Rights Act of 1964 had a profound and enduring impact on global human rights movements, international perceptions of the

United States, and international norms of equality and justice. Its passage inspired liberation movements, fostered solidarity and internationalism, and influenced the development of international human rights law and norms. The legacy of the Civil Rights Act continues to inspire movements for justice and equality around the world, reminding us of the universal struggle for human rights and the importance of standing up against racism, discrimination, and injustice in all its forms.

Chapter 12: Unfinished Business

Despite the significant progress made since the passage of the Civil Rights Act of 1964, the struggle for racial equality in the United States remains far from over. This chapter delves into the ongoing challenges and disparities in achieving full equality, explores modern-day manifestations of racial discrimination and inequality, and discusses the calls for continued activism and legislative action to address the unfinished business of the civil rights movement.

Ongoing Challenges and Disparities in Achieving Full Equality

1. Persistent Racial Disparities: Racial disparities continue to pervade nearly every aspect of American life, including education, employment, healthcare, housing, and criminal justice. African Americans and other marginalized communities face disproportionate rates of poverty, unemployment, and incarceration, highlighting the systemic barriers to equality that persist.

2. Educational Inequities: Despite efforts to desegregate schools and promote equal access to education, educational inequities persist along racial lines. Minority students are more likely to attend under-resourced schools with fewer opportunities for academic achievement, perpetuating cycles of poverty and disadvantage.

3. Economic Inequality: Economic inequality remains a pressing issue, with minority communities facing higher rates of poverty, unemployment, and wealth disparity compared to their white counterparts. Structural barriers to economic opportunity, such as discriminatory hiring practices and lack of access to capital, hinder upward mobility and perpetuate socioeconomic disparities.

4. Healthcare Disparities: Racial and ethnic minorities experience disparities in access to healthcare, quality of care, and health outcomes. African Americans, Hispanics, and Native Americans are more likely to lack health insurance coverage, receive lower-quality healthcare services, and suffer from higher rates of chronic diseases such as diabetes, hypertension, and cancer.

5. Criminal Justice System Inequities: The criminal justice system disproportionately impacts communities of color, with African Americans and

Hispanics overrepresented at every stage of the criminal justice process, from arrest and prosecution to sentencing and incarceration. Racial profiling, biased policing practices, and discriminatory sentencing policies contribute to the overcriminalization and mass incarceration of minority populations.

Modern-Day Manifestations of Racial Discrimination and Inequality

1. Police Brutality and Systemic Racism: Incidents of police brutality and systemic racism continue to occur, sparking protests and calls for police reform and accountability. High-profile cases of police violence against unarmed Black individuals, such as the deaths of George Floyd, Breonna Taylor, and Ahmaud Arbery, have reignited national conversations about racial justice and police accountability.

2. Voter Suppression and Disenfranchisement: Efforts to suppress minority voter turnout and disenfranchise marginalized communities persist, posing significant challenges to democracy and equal representation. Voter suppression tactics such as strict voter ID laws, gerrymandering, and voter purges disproportionately affect African American, Hispanic, and Indigenous voters, undermining the principles of free and fair elections.

3. Housing Discrimination and Segregation: Housing discrimination and segregation remain pervasive, with minority communities facing barriers to access affordable housing and opportunity-rich neighborhoods. Discriminatory lending practices, redlining, and exclusionary zoning policies perpetuate residential segregation and exacerbate racial disparities in housing quality, stability, and wealth accumulation.

4. Educational Opportunity Gaps: Educational opportunity gaps persist, with minority students disproportionately attending underfunded schools with limited resources and opportunities for academic success. Persistent disparities in educational attainment and achievement contribute to the perpetuation of socioeconomic inequality and hinder upward mobility for minority youth.

5. Environmental Injustice: Environmental injustice disproportionately impacts communities of color, with African American, Hispanic, and Indigenous communities bearing the brunt of environmental pollution, toxic waste sites, and environmental hazards. Environmental racism perpetuates health disparities and

exacerbates socioeconomic inequality, further marginalizing already vulnerable populations.

Calls for Continued Activism and Legislative Action

1. Community Mobilization and Grassroots Organizing: Continued activism and grassroots organizing are essential for addressing the unfinished business of the civil rights movement. Community-led efforts to mobilize, educate, and advocate for racial justice and equality play a crucial role in raising awareness, building coalitions, and effecting meaningful change at the local, state, and national levels.

2. Legislative Reforms and Policy Solutions: Legislative reforms and policy solutions are needed to address the root causes of racial discrimination and inequality and advance the cause of racial justice. Comprehensive legislative initiatives, such as police reform, criminal justice reform, voting rights protection, and economic equity measures, can help dismantle systemic barriers to equality and promote greater social and economic inclusion for all Americans.

3. Corporate Accountability and Social Responsibility: Corporations and businesses have a role to play in advancing racial equity and social justice through corporate accountability and social responsibility initiatives. Investing in diverse leadership, equitable hiring practices, and community development programs can help promote diversity, equity, and inclusion in the workplace and society at large.

4. Education and Awareness: Education and awareness are essential tools for combating racism and promoting understanding, empathy, and solidarity across racial and ethnic lines. Promoting multicultural education, anti-racism training, and critical dialogue about race and privilege can help foster a more inclusive and equitable society where all individuals are valued and respected.

5. Intersectional Advocacy and Allyship: Intersectional advocacy and allyship are critical for building coalitions and amplifying the voices of marginalized communities in the fight for racial justice. Recognizing the interconnectedness of racial, gender, economic, and social justice issues and standing in solidarity with those most affected by systemic oppression can help create a more unified and effective movement for change.

In conclusion, the unfinished business of the civil rights movement requires sustained activism, legislative action, and social change efforts to address the ongoing challenges and disparities in achieving full equality. Modern-day manifestations of racial discrimination and inequality underscore the urgent need for systemic reforms and transformative solutions to advance the cause of racial justice. Calls for continued activism and legislative action resonate with the enduring legacy of the civil rights movement, reminding us of the collective responsibility to build a more just, equitable, and inclusive society for all.

Chapter 13: Commemorating the Civil Rights Act

The Civil Rights Act of 1964 stands as a landmark piece of legislation in American history, marking a pivotal moment in the struggle for equality and justice. This chapter explores the various ways in which the Civil Rights Act is commemorated, reflects on its significance in American history, and discusses efforts to preserve and promote awareness of civil rights history.

Commemorative Events and Anniversaries Honoring the Civil Rights Act

1. Civil Rights Anniversaries: Every year, communities across the United States commemorate the anniversaries of key milestones in the civil rights movement, including the passage of the Civil Rights Act of 1964. These anniversaries serve as opportunities to reflect on the progress made, honor the sacrifices of civil rights leaders and activists, and recommit to the ongoing struggle for racial equality.

2. Martin Luther King Jr. Day: Martin Luther King Jr. Day, observed on the third Monday of January, commemorates the life and legacy of Dr. Martin Luther King Jr., a central figure in the civil rights movement. The holiday is marked by events such as marches, rallies, and service projects that celebrate King's vision of a beloved community and his commitment to nonviolent resistance and social justice.

3. Civil Rights Museums and Memorials: Civil rights museums and memorials, such as the National Civil Rights Museum in Memphis, Tennessee, and the National Museum of African American History and Culture in Washington, D.C., serve as important venues for commemorating the Civil Rights Act and preserving the history of the civil rights movement. These institutions provide educational resources, exhibits, and programs that illuminate the struggles and triumphs of the movement and inspire future generations to continue the fight for justice.

4. Commemorative Marches and Events: Commemorative marches, events, and ceremonies are held in cities and communities across the country to honor the legacy of the civil rights movement and the passage of the Civil Rights Act.

These events often feature speeches, performances, and panel discussions that highlight the significance of the act and its impact on American society.

5. Educational Initiatives: Educational initiatives and programs are launched to commemorate the Civil Rights Act and educate the public about its historical context, significance, and legacy. Schools, universities, and community organizations may organize workshops, lectures, and film screenings that explore the history of the civil rights movement and its relevance to contemporary issues of social justice and equality.

Reflections on the Significance of the Act in American History

1. Milestone in Civil Rights Struggle: The Civil Rights Act of 1964 is widely recognized as a milestone in the civil rights struggle, representing a turning point in America's long and tumultuous journey toward racial equality and justice. Its passage marked the culmination of years of grassroots organizing, protest, and advocacy by civil rights leaders and activists across the country.

2. Expanding the Promise of Equality: The Civil Rights Act expanded the promise of equality and freedom enshrined in the Declaration of Independence and the Constitution to include all Americans, regardless of race, color, religion, sex, or national origin. It affirmed the principles of equal protection under the law and non-discrimination, laying the groundwork for future civil rights legislation and judicial decisions.

3. Transformation of American Society: The Civil Rights Act transformed American society by dismantling legal segregation and discrimination and opening up new opportunities for African Americans and other marginalized communities. It paved the way for greater social and economic inclusion, increased political participation, and the emergence of more inclusive and multicultural communities.

4. Legacy of Courage and Resilience: The Civil Rights Act stands as a testament to the courage and resilience of the countless individuals who fought tirelessly for justice and equality in the face of adversity. From civil rights leaders and activists to ordinary citizens who risked their lives to challenge injustice, the legacy of the civil rights movement continues to inspire and empower future generations to stand up for what is right.

5. Ongoing Struggle for Equality: While the Civil Rights Act represented a significant step forward in the struggle for equality, it also served as a reminder of the ongoing challenges and disparities that persist in American society. The act's passage did not magically eradicate racism or eliminate inequality, but rather laid the foundation for continued efforts to address systemic injustice and promote greater equity and inclusion for all Americans.

Efforts to Preserve and Promote Awareness of Civil Rights History

1. Historic Preservation and Documentation: Efforts are underway to preserve and document historic sites, landmarks, and artifacts associated with the civil rights movement, ensuring that future generations have access to the tangible and intangible heritage of the struggle for equality. Historic preservation organizations, museums, and archives work to safeguard and promote awareness of civil rights history through research, conservation, and public programming.

2. Digital Archives and Oral Histories: Digital archives and oral history projects play a crucial role in preserving and disseminating the stories and voices of civil rights activists and participants. Online platforms and repositories provide access to primary source materials, interviews, photographs, and audiovisual recordings that document the lived experiences and contributions of individuals involved in the civil rights movement.

3. Curriculum Development and Educational Resources: Curriculum development and educational resources are designed to incorporate civil rights history into K-12 schools, colleges, and universities, ensuring that students learn about the struggles and achievements of the civil rights movement as part of their formal education. Lesson plans, teaching guides, and multimedia materials help educators engage students in critical dialogue about race, equality, and social justice.

4. Community Engagement and Dialogue: Community engagement and dialogue initiatives foster conversations about civil rights history and its relevance to contemporary issues of racial justice and equality. Community-based organizations, libraries, and cultural institutions host public forums, discussion groups, and film screenings that encourage dialogue, reflection, and collective action around civil rights themes.

5. Interdisciplinary Research and Scholarship: Interdisciplinary research and scholarship contribute to our understanding of civil rights history and its enduring legacy in American society. Scholars, historians, and activists explore the intersectional dimensions of the civil rights movement, examining its connections to other social justice struggles and its impact on law, politics, culture, and identity.

In conclusion, the Civil Rights Act of 1964 is commemorated through a variety of events, initiatives, and programs that honor its legacy, reflect on its significance, and promote awareness of civil rights history. From annual commemorations and educational initiatives to historic preservation efforts and community engagement activities, these efforts serve to ensure that the lessons and legacies of the civil rights movement are preserved and passed down to future generations. As we commemorate the Civil Rights Act, we are reminded of the ongoing struggle for equality and justice and the collective responsibility to continue the fight for civil rights and human rights for all.

Chapter 14: Contemporary Perspectives

The legacy of the Civil Rights Act of 1964 continues to shape contemporary perspectives on issues of race, equality, and justice in the United States. This chapter explores the diverse range of contemporary perspectives on the legacy and relevance of the Civil Rights Act, examines intersectional analyses of race, gender, and other forms of discrimination, and discusses the challenges and opportunities for advancing civil rights in the 21st century.

Contemporary Perspectives on the Legacy and Relevance of the Civil Rights Act

1. Historical Significance: Many view the Civil Rights Act as a defining moment in American history, marking the culmination of decades of struggle against racial segregation and discrimination. Its legacy is celebrated as a testament to the power of collective action and the resilience of those who fought for equality and justice.

2. Legal Precedent: Legal scholars and practitioners recognize the Civil Rights Act as a foundational document in the development of civil rights law in the United States. Its provisions on non-discrimination, equal protection under the law, and the right to freedom from racial discrimination have shaped the jurisprudence of the courts and continue to influence legal interpretations and decisions.

3. Symbol of Progress: For many Americans, the Civil Rights Act symbolizes progress toward a more inclusive and equitable society. Its passage represents a turning point in the nation's history, signaling a commitment to the principles of equality, justice, and democracy enshrined in the Constitution.

4. Unfinished Business: Others view the Civil Rights Act as unfinished business, highlighting the ongoing challenges and disparities that persist in American society. While the act was a significant step forward in the struggle for racial equality, it did not eradicate racism or eliminate systemic injustice, leaving much work to be done to achieve full equality and inclusion for all.

5. Legacy of Activism: Contemporary activists and social justice advocates draw inspiration from the civil rights movement and the legacy of the Civil

Rights Act in their efforts to address pressing issues of racial inequality, police brutality, voting rights, and economic justice. The spirit of grassroots organizing, nonviolent resistance, and collective action continues to inform contemporary movements for change.

Intersectional Analyses of Race, Gender, and Other Forms of Discrimination

1. Intersectionality Theory: Intersectionality theory, pioneered by legal scholar Kimberlé Crenshaw, examines how multiple forms of oppression and discrimination intersect and compound to shape individuals' experiences and identities. Intersectional analyses of race, gender, class, sexuality, and other axes of identity illuminate the complex and interconnected nature of systemic inequality and injustice.

2. Race and Gender: Intersectional analyses of race and gender highlight the unique challenges faced by women of color in navigating systems of oppression and discrimination. Women of color experience intersecting forms of racism and sexism that shape their experiences in distinct ways, often resulting in compounded disadvantages and barriers to equality.

3. LGBTQ+ Rights: Intersectional perspectives on civil rights encompass issues of sexual orientation and gender identity, recognizing the intersecting forms of discrimination faced by LGBTQ+ individuals, particularly those who are also marginalized by race, ethnicity, or socioeconomic status. Efforts to advance LGBTQ+ rights are intertwined with broader struggles for equality and inclusion.

4. Disability Rights: Disability rights advocacy intersects with civil rights activism, as individuals with disabilities confront systemic barriers to access, inclusion, and participation in society. Intersectional analyses of disability rights recognize the intersecting forms of discrimination faced by people with disabilities, particularly those from marginalized communities.

5. Immigrant Rights: Immigrant rights activism intersects with civil rights advocacy, as immigrant communities confront discrimination, xenophobia, and anti-immigrant policies. Intersectional analyses of immigrant rights highlight the intersecting forms of oppression faced by immigrant individuals and families,

particularly those who are also marginalized by race, ethnicity, or socioeconomic status.

Challenges and Opportunities for Advancing Civil Rights in the 21st Century

1. Systemic Racism: Addressing systemic racism remains a central challenge for advancing civil rights in the 21st century. Structural inequalities in areas such as education, employment, housing, and criminal justice perpetuate racial disparities and hinder progress toward racial equality and justice.

2. Voting Rights: Protecting voting rights and combating voter suppression are critical priorities for advancing civil rights in the 21st century. Efforts to restrict access to the ballot box disproportionately impact minority communities and undermine the democratic principles of equal representation and participation.

3. Criminal Justice Reform: Reforming the criminal justice system is essential for advancing civil rights and addressing issues of police brutality, mass incarceration, and racial disparities in law enforcement. Calls for police reform, ending qualified immunity, and investing in community-based alternatives to incarceration are central to this effort.

4. Economic Justice: Advancing economic justice is integral to the struggle for civil rights, as economic inequalities perpetuate racial disparities and exacerbate social inequality. Efforts to address income inequality, create job opportunities, and promote economic mobility for marginalized communities are essential for achieving greater equity and inclusion.

5. Intersectional Advocacy: Embracing intersectional perspectives and approaches is vital for advancing civil rights in the 21st century. Recognizing the interconnectedness of race, gender, class, sexuality, and other axes of identity helps to center the experiences and needs of marginalized communities and build more inclusive and effective movements for social change.

In conclusion, contemporary perspectives on the legacy and relevance of the Civil Rights Act encompass a range of viewpoints, from celebrations of progress to calls for continued action to address unfinished business. Intersectional analyses of race, gender, and other forms of discrimination illuminate the complex nature of systemic inequality and injustice in the United States. Despite the challenges that remain, the Civil Rights Act continues to inspire efforts to advance civil rights and promote greater equality, justice, and inclusion for all Americans in the 21st century.

Chapter 15: Conclusion

As we conclude our exploration of the Civil Rights Act of 1964 and its legacy, it is essential to reflect on the key themes and takeaways that have emerged throughout our journey. From the historical context of racial discrimination to contemporary perspectives on civil rights, the Civil Rights Act continues to shape our understanding of equality, justice, and the ongoing struggle for racial equity in the United States. This chapter provides a summary of key themes and takeaways, reflects on the enduring impact of the Civil Rights Act, and issues a call to action for continued progress toward equality and justice.

Summary of Key Themes and Takeaways

1. Historical Context of Racial Discrimination: The Civil Rights Act emerged from a long history of racial discrimination and oppression in the United States, including slavery, segregation, and Jim Crow laws. It was a response to the systemic inequalities and injustices that African Americans and other marginalized communities faced in virtually every aspect of life.

2. Legislative Achievement and Political Mobilization: The passage of the Civil Rights Act represented a significant legislative achievement and a triumph of political mobilization and grassroots activism. It was the result of years of struggle, sacrifice, and collective action by civil rights leaders, activists, and ordinary citizens who demanded an end to racial segregation and discrimination.

3. Expanding the Promise of Equality: The Civil Rights Act expanded the promise of equality and justice enshrined in the Constitution to include all Americans, regardless of race, color, religion, sex, or national origin. It affirmed the principles of equal protection under the law and non-discrimination, laying the groundwork for future civil rights legislation and judicial decisions.

4. Legacy of Courage and Resilience: The Civil Rights Act stands as a testament to the courage and resilience of those who fought tirelessly for justice and equality in the face of adversity. From civil rights leaders and activists to ordinary citizens who risked their lives to challenge injustice, the legacy of the civil rights movement continues to inspire and empower future generations.

5. Intersectional Analyses of Discrimination: Intersectional analyses of race, gender, and other forms of discrimination illuminate the complex and interconnected nature of systemic inequality and injustice. Recognizing the intersecting dimensions of oppression faced by marginalized communities is essential for understanding the full scope of the civil rights struggle and advancing a more inclusive and equitable society.

6. Challenges and Opportunities for Advancing Civil Rights: Despite the progress made since the passage of the Civil Rights Act, significant challenges and disparities persist in American society. Addressing systemic racism, protecting voting rights, reforming the criminal justice system, advancing economic justice, and embracing intersectional advocacy are critical priorities for advancing civil rights in the 21st century.

Reflections on the Enduring Impact of the Civil Rights Act

The enduring impact of the Civil Rights Act can be seen in its profound influence on American law, politics, and society. It remains a symbol of progress and a beacon of hope for those who continue to fight for equality and justice. The act's legacy is felt in every aspect of American life, from the desegregation of public spaces to the expansion of civil rights protections for marginalized communities. Its principles of non-discrimination, equal protection under the law, and the right to freedom from racial discrimination have shaped the nation's understanding of civil rights and human rights, serving as a touchstone for future generations of activists and advocates.

Call to Action for Continued Progress Toward Equality and Justice

As we reflect on the legacy of the Civil Rights Act, we are reminded of the unfinished business of the civil rights movement and the ongoing struggle for racial equity in the United States. It is incumbent upon all of us to continue the work of advancing civil rights and promoting greater equality, justice, and inclusion for all Americans. This requires a collective commitment to challenging systemic racism, dismantling barriers to opportunity, and amplifying the voices of marginalized communities.

We must engage in intersectional advocacy that recognizes the interconnected nature of oppression and centers the experiences and needs of those most affected by systemic inequality. We must protect and expand voting rights, reform the criminal justice system, address economic disparities, and ensure access to quality education, healthcare, and housing for all. We must confront prejudice and discrimination in all its forms and build bridges of understanding and solidarity across racial, ethnic, gender, and socioeconomic lines.

In conclusion, the Civil Rights Act of 1964 stands as a testament to the power of collective action and the resilience of those who have fought for justice and equality throughout history. Its legacy reminds us of the enduring importance of the struggle for civil rights and the ongoing quest for a more just, equitable, and inclusive society. As we look to the future, let us heed the lessons of the past and continue the march toward freedom, dignity, and equality for all.

Appendix: Key Documents

In this appendix, we provide excerpts from the Civil Rights Act of 1964, along with relevant speeches, court decisions, legislative records, and additional resources for further reading and research. These documents offer insights into the historical context, legal framework, and political significance of the Civil Rights Act, as well as its enduring impact on American society.

Excerpts from the Civil Rights Act of 1964

The Civil Rights Act of 1964 is a comprehensive piece of legislation that prohibits discrimination on the basis of race, color, religion, sex, or national origin and protects the civil rights of all Americans. The following excerpts highlight key provisions of the act:

1. Title I: Voting Rights

- "No person shall be denied the right to vote in any Federal, State, or local election because of race, color, or previous condition of servitude."

2. Title II: Public Accommodations

- "All persons shall be entitled to the full and equal enjoyment of the goods, services, facilities, privileges, advantages, and accommodations of any place of public accommodation, as defined in this section, without discrimination or segregation on the ground of race, color, religion, or national origin."

3. Title III: Desegregation of Public Facilities

- "No person shall (a) withhold, deny, or attempt to withhold or deny, or deprive or attempt to deprive, any person of any right or privilege secured by section 201 or 202, or (b) intimidate, threaten, or coerce, or attempt to intimidate, threaten, or coerce any person with the purpose of interfering with any right or privilege secured by section 201 or 202, or (c) punish or attempt to punish any person for exercising or attempting to exercise any right or privilege secured by section 201 or 202."

4. Title IV: Desegregation of Public Education

- "No person in the United States shall, on the ground of race, color, or national origin, be excluded from participation in, be denied the benefits of, or be subjected to discrimination under any program or activity receiving Federal financial assistance."

5. Title V: Commission on Civil Rights

- "There is hereby established a Commission on Civil Rights (hereinafter referred to as the 'Commission') consisting of eight members, not more than four of whom shall at any one time be of the same political party."

Relevant Speeches, Court Decisions, and Legislative Records

1. Martin Luther King Jr., "I Have a Dream" Speech (1963): Martin Luther King Jr.'s iconic speech delivered during the March on Washington for Jobs and Freedom on August 28, 1963, called for an end to racial discrimination and segregation and advocated for civil rights legislation.

2. Brown v. Board of Education (1954): The landmark Supreme Court decision in Brown v. Board of Education declared state laws establishing separate public schools for black and white students unconstitutional, overturning the doctrine of "separate but equal" and laying the groundwork for desegregation.

3. Southern Manifesto (1956): The Southern Manifesto was a document signed by 101 members of Congress in opposition to racial integration and the Supreme Court's decision in Brown v. Board of Education. It expressed support for continued segregation and resistance to civil rights reforms.

4. Civil Rights Act of 1957: The Civil Rights Act of 1957 was the first federal civil rights legislation passed since Reconstruction. It aimed to protect the voting rights of African Americans and established the U.S. Commission on Civil Rights to investigate allegations of voter discrimination.

5. 1964 Democratic National Convention Speech by Fannie Lou Hamer: Fannie Lou Hamer, a civil rights activist and leader in the Mississippi Freedom Democratic Party, delivered a powerful speech at the 1964 Democratic National Convention, challenging the party's commitment to racial justice and demanding equal representation for African Americans.

Additional Resources for Further Reading and Research

1. Books
   - "Parting the Waters: America in the King Years 1954-63" by Taylor Branch
   - "Freedom Riders: 1961 and the Struggle for Racial Justice" by Raymond Arsenault
   - "The Warmth of Other Suns: The Epic Story of America's Great Migration" by Isabel Wilkerson
   - "At the Dark End of the Street: Black Women, Rape, and Resistance—A New History of the Civil Rights Movement from Rosa Parks to the Rise of Black Power" by Danielle L. McGuire

2. Documentaries
   - "Eyes on the Prize" (PBS documentary series)
   - "13th" (Netflix documentary film)
   - "The African Americans: Many Rivers to Cross with Henry Louis Gates Jr." (PBS documentary series)

3. Websites and Online Archives
   - The Martin Luther King Jr. Research and Education Institute at Stanford University: https://kinginstitute.stanford.edu/
   - The National Civil Rights Museum: https://www.civilrightsmuseum.org/
   - The Library of Congress, Civil Rights History Project: https://www.loc.gov/collections/civil-rights-history-project/about-this-collection/

4. Academic Journals
   - The Journal of African American History
   - The Journal of Civil Rights and Economic Development
   - The Journal of Southern History

5. Educational Resources
   - Teaching Tolerance: https://www.tolerance.org/
   - Zinn Education Project: https://www.zinnedproject.org/
   - Facing History and Ourselves: https://www.facinghistory.org/

By engaging with these key documents, speeches, court decisions, and legislative records, along with additional resources for further reading and research, readers can deepen their understanding of the Civil Rights Act of 1964 and its historical context, legal significance, and enduring impact on American society. These resources provide valuable insights into the ongoing struggle for civil rights and the quest for equality and justice for all Americans.

Don't miss out!

Visit the website below and you can sign up to receive emails whenever Michael Johnson publishes a new book. There's no charge and no obligation.

https://books2read.com/r/B-A-OREFB-IBWAD

Did you love *The Civil Rights Act*? Then you should read *The Harlem Renaissance*[1] by Michael Johnson!

"Renaissance of the Harlem: Cultural Awakening in the African American Community" delves into the transformative era of the Harlem Renaissance, illuminating its origins, luminaries, and enduring legacy. From the influx of African Americans during the Great Migration to the emergence of literary giants like Langston Hughes and Zora Neale Hurston, this book explores the vibrant intersections of art, music, theater, and activism that defined Harlem in the early 20th century. With insightful analyses and profiles of key figures, it celebrates the cultural resurgence while acknowledging its complexities and challenges, offering a compelling narrative of empowerment and inspiration.

---

1. https://books2read.com/u/b6JjyZ

2. https://books2read.com/u/b6JjyZ

About the Author

Michael Johnson is a distinguished historian specializing in American history. With a degree in History from Harvard University, Johnson's work delves into pivotal moments, figures, and themes shaping the United States. He has authored numerous acclaimed books, offering insightful perspectives and engaging narratives. Johnson's commitment to meticulous scholarship and compelling storytelling has earned him widespread acclaim in the field. Passionate about sharing his expertise, he frequently engages in lectures and public events to foster a deeper appreciation for America's past.